Das kleine blaue Flugzeug
Peter the plane

discovers the rainbow
entdeckt den Regenbogen

Anja Offelder

This book
belongs to:

Dieses Buch
gehört:

written by Anja Offelder
Thank you to Jennifer Lavan, J. R. Finlayson, Allan and Tony

Manufactured and published by
Books on Demand GmbH, Norderstedt, Germany
ISBN: 9783839150795

**For
Isabella**

*Für
Isabella*

Once upon a time…

**there was a little blue aeroplane.
His name was Peter.**

Es war einmal...

*ein kleines blaues
Flugzeug namens Peter...*

He was very sad and he cried and cried.

He cried so much because he had spent five years all alone in a small hangar on the king's airport and nobody visited him or paid him any attention.

Es war sehr traurig und es weinte und weinte große Kullertränen.

Und es jammerte, weil es nun schon seit fünf Jahren ganz alleine in der kleinen Garage auf dem königlichen Flughafen stand und niemand es mehr beachtete oder gar besuchte.

One day a little fairy called Fiona appeared
and heard the crying in the hangar.

"Oh dear" she said.
"Who is crying so bitterly?"

*Eines Tages kam Fiona, die kleine Wetterfee,
vorbei geflogen und hörte das Weinen aus
der Garage.*

*Nanu, dachte sie. Wer weint denn
da so bitterlich?*

She went inside and found the little blue propeller plane. "Hello little plane. What is the matter with you? Why are you crying?" asked the little fairy.

"Who are you?" the little blue plane sighed. "I am Fiona the little monsoon fairy."

Sie flog hinein und fand
das kleine blaue Propellerflugzeug.
»Hallo, kleines Flugzeug!
Was ist denn los mit Dir?
Warum weinst Du denn so?«,
fragte die kleine Fee.

»Wer bist Du denn?«,
schluchzte das kleine blaue Flugzeug.
»Ich bin Fiona, die Wetterfee«,
sagte die kleine Fee.

"Oh my dear monsoon fairy!
I am so sad, oh so sad, because the king
does not come to visit me anymore and he
does not fly with me anymore either."

"The king?" asked the little fairy.

*»Ach, liebe Wetterfee, ich bin so traurig,
sooo traurig, weil der König mich gar nicht
mehr besuchen kommt und auch nicht mehr
mit mir fliegt!«*

»Der König?«, fragte die kleine Wetterfee.

"Yes, the king" said Peter.
"King Mandolin of Chocolasia who lives in the golden castle with the almond windows" answered Peter the plane.

»Ja, König Mandolin von Schokoladien, der im goldenen Schloss mit den Mandelfenstern wohnt«, antwortete Peter, das kleine blaue Flugzeug.

"Ah, so king Mandolin doesn't come and visit you anymore. Why not?"

"He has bought this new-fangled silver jet plane. Now he only flies with it and he doesn't even think about me anymore!"

»So ,so. Der König kommt dich also nicht mehr besuchen?«
»Nein«, antwortete das kleine blaue Flugzeug.

»Seitdem er diesen neumodischen Düsenjet hat, fliegt er nur noch mit dem schicken silbernen Jet zu seinen Terminen und an mich denkt niemand mehr!

"I have been standing for over five years in this boring, boring dusty hangar. I am so lonely and I long to fly again.

Today the king has an important appointment and just passed me by on the way to his silver jet, without even waving", sighed Peter the propeller plane.
Big tears run down his cheeks.

Nun stehe ich schon seit fünf Jahren hier in dieser langweiligen, verstaubten Garage herum und bin so alleine. Dabei möchte ich doch so gerne noch mal fliegen!

Heute hat der König offensichtlich wieder einen wichtigen Termin, denn eben fuhr er wieder an mir vorbei zu seinem silbernen Jet. Er hat mir nicht einmal gewinkt«, schluchzte Peter, das kleine blaue Flugzeug. Dicke Tränen kullerten über seine Wangen.

Fiona thought for one moment and then she said: "But that's terrible!
Oh you poor poor little plane!
Don't be sad. I can help you.
I have a theory because I am the monsoon fairy!"

Then Fiona cast a spell –
a very special weather spell:

Fiona dachte eine Weile nach. Dann sagte sie: »Oh je, das ist ja schrecklich!
Ach, Du armes kleines Flugzeug! Sei nicht traurig, ich kann Dir helfen.

Ich habe eine Idee, denn ich bin die Wetterfee!«

Und Fiona versuchte einen Wetterfeen-Zauberspruch:

"Abracadabra...!
I am the monsoon fairy called Fiona!
I come from the holy island of Iona!
I can make sun, rain, storm and snow, but
my favourite trick is to make a rainbow!
But what we need here to help
Peter the plane
is very easy to explain:
We need plenty of snow
in a magic show:
Snowflakes and hailstones shall fall
from the sky,
to cover the jet - can you guess why?
The new-fangled jet will be covered in ice,
it can no longer fly but it will look so nice!
Abracadabra and thanks to the snow,
I am the fairy of the rainbow!"

»Simsalabim, ich bin die Wetterfee.
Ich zaubere vom Himmel ganz viel Schnee.
Auch Hagel und Eiszapfen soll es regnen,
die sollen dem silbernen Jet begegnen.
Und der Schneesturm deckt im Nu
den Düsenjet des Königs zu!
Simsalabim und Dank an den Schnee,
ich bin die kleine Wetterfee!«

The spell worked.

Fiona made snow and ice appear.

Es hatte geklappt!

Fiona hatte Eis und Schnee gezaubert.

In a flash the silver jet had disappeared
under a mountain of snow and ice.
Thick icicles hung from the wings.
The windows were covered in ice
so thick that the king was no longer
able to look out of the cockpit windows.

"Oh dear! Oh dear!" shouted the king.
"What shall I do now? I am in such a hurry
and I must be at my next court
appointment urgently!"

*Und im Nu war das silberne Düsenflugzeug
zugeschneit! An seinen Tragflächen hingen
dicke Eiszapfen und auch die Fenster waren
voller Eis, so dass der König nicht mehr aus
dem Cockpitfenster sehen konnte.*

*»Oh je, oh je!«, rief König Mandolin.
»Was mache ich denn jetzt? Ich habe es doch
so eilig und muss ganz dringend zu meinem
wichtigen Termin!«*

Then he suddenly remembered his little
blue propeller plane.
"But just a moment…
Thank goodness! Of course!
I still have my little blue propeller plane.

It's still standing in the royal hangar and
will therefore be free of ice and snow. I'll
just have to fly with it!"

*Da erinnerte er sich plötzlich an sein kleines
blaues Propellerflugzeug.*

*»Ach, ich hab ja noch das kleine blaue
Flugzeug! Es steht doch in der königlichen
Garage. Da kann es nicht vereist und nicht
zugeschneit sein. Dann muss ich eben mit
diesem fliegen!«*

The king strode into the royal hangar and the little blue plane was overcome with pleasure. He was so happy and so excited that his propellers started to spin.

"Hello your Majesty! I can see you are in a hurry. We can leave any time. I am ready for takeoff!"

Der König ging in die Garage und das kleine blaue Flugzeug freute sich riesig.
Vor lauter Freude brummte es schon mit seinen Propellern.

»Hallo König!«, rief es aufgeregt.
»Ich bin startklar!
Ready for takeoff!«

"Thank goodness!"
exclaimed the king.

"I am in such a hurry!"

»Gott sei Dank!«,
rief der König.

»Ich habe es doch so eilig!«

He jumped in and they took off immediately.

The little plane was so happy that he flew higher and higher and very fast. He was so pleased that he danced on the clouds…

Er stieg ein und sie flogen gleich los.

Das kleine blaue Flugzeug war so glücklich, dass es ganz schnell flog und immer höher; und es freute sich so sehr, dass es in den Wolken tanzte...

...and the monsoon fairy flew alongside and with a magic spell she created a lovely colourful rainbow in the sky.

"Look! Look your Majesty!
A rainbow!" shouted Peter joyfully!

"Oh, how wonderful" said King Mandolin.

...und die Wetterfee flog neben ihnen her und zauberte einen schönen bunten Regenbogen für die beiden an den Himmel.

»Schau mal König: ein Regenbogen!«, lachte das kleine blaue Flugzeug.

»Ach, wie schön«, sagte König Mandolin.

"Sire!" called out the little blue plane.
"Look over there! There is my friend,
Fiona, the little monsoon fairy.
She created the rainbow."
"Do you think she would tell us how she
does it?" asked the king. Peter waved to
her with his wings.

"Hello Fiona! Would you mind telling us
how you make rainbows?" he asked.

*»König!«, rief das kleine blaue Flugzeug.
»Da fliegt meine Freundin Fiona, die
Wetterfee! Sie hat den Regenbogen
gezaubert.«*
*»Ob sie uns wohl verrät, wie sie das macht?«,
fragte der König. Peter winkte der Fee mit
seinen Flügeln.*

*»Hallo Fiona! Verrätst Du uns, wie man
einen Regenbogen macht?«, rief Peter.*

Fiona laughed.
"I have a magic wand that's as light as a feather,
because I am the fairy who controls the weather.
If you would like to know,
how I make the rainbow
just watch and follow my lead,
a few short steps to what we need:

Basil, rosemary and lime:
We need sunshine and rain at the same time,
and the sun must be behind you,
below the magic angle of fourty two!"

Fiona lachte:
»Oh, ich bin die kleine Wetterfee,
ich habe einen langen Zeh.
Ich will Euch verraten,
wie ich den Regenbogen mache,
denn das ist eine ganz einfache Sache.

"With a splash of rain and a dash of sun,
coming together all as one.
The sunrays are shining through
the falling raindrop just for you.

And whenever sunrays and raindrops unite
a rainbow appears - in a colourful light.
Look! Can you see it all so bright -
it's not magic, it's the physics of light!"

*Man braucht Sonne und Regen zur selben
Zeit,
und dann ist schon alles bereit:
Wenn nun die Sonnenstrahlen durch die
Regentropfen scheinen
und sich Sonnenlicht und Wasser vereinen,
dann entsteht – es ist nicht gelogen –
ein wunderschöner Regenbogen!*

*Zauberei ist das nicht,
sondern die Physik vom Licht,
wenn sich der Sonnenstrahl
im Regenwasser bricht.*

Now that you know how a rainbow is made,
I'll tell you the colours- shade by shade:

(let's take it from the top)
Red, orange, yellow and green,
such lovely shades to be seen.
Followed by blue, indigo and violet,
that's all the colours your eyes will get."

Auch die Farben will ich Dir nennen.
Ich denke Du wirst sie alle kennen:

Oben kommt Rot,
es folgt Orange,
dann Gelb und Grün:
eine schöne Melange!
Nun kommen Blau und Violett
und fertig ist das Farben-Set!

If you see a rainbow or a shooting star,
I hope you know just how lucky you are.
The legend says:
They open the gates
to fairy tale land,
so make your wish and raise your hand,
towards the rainbow or the shooting star,
it doesn't matter where you are:
The fairies will see you
and make your wish come true!

Und wenn Du einen Regenbogen siehst,
sich Dir das Tor zur Märchenwelt
aufschließt.
Denn die Legende sagt:
Siehst Du Regenbögen, Sternschnuppen oder
Nymphen,
dann darfst Du Dir ganz heimlich etwas
wünschen!«

"Thank you Fiona!"
shouted Peter and the king.

"Well" sighed the king, "I had completely
forgotten how good it feels to fly with my
little propeller plane. This is really fun!
From this day forth we shall fly together
every Sunday!" proclaimed the king.

*»Danke Fiona!«, riefen Peter und König
Mandolin.*

*»Ach«, seufzte der König. »Ich hatte ganz
vergessen, wie schön es ist, mit dem
Propellerflugzeug zu fliegen.
Es macht mir richtig Spaß, mit Dir
zu fliegen, Peter. Ab heute werde ich
jeden Sonntag einen Ausflug mit
Dir machen, mein kleines blaues
Propellerflugzeug!«, verkündete der König.*

"Oh how wonderful" said Peter the little blue plane.

He was so very proud and so happy, that he grinned from wing tip to wing tip!

»Oh wie schön«, sagte das kleine Propellerflugzeug.

Es war sehr stolz und überglücklich, so dass es von einer Tragfläche bis zur anderen grinste.

From that day on, King Mandolin and Peter the propeller plane were inseparable. Every Sunday they would fly around the kingdom of Chocolasia.

Fiona the little monsoon fairy would always surprise them with a stunning rainbow.

Von diesem Tag an waren König Mandolin und das kleine blaue Propellerflugzeug unzertrennlich.
Und wenn sie nicht gestorben sind, dann machen sie noch heute jeden Sonntag einen Ausflug.

Und die kleine Wetterfee Fiona zaubert ihnen immer einen Regenbogen an den Himmel...

And off they went to fairyland.

The end.

...auf dem Weg ins Märchenland...

Ende

Colour your own rainbow!

Regenbögen zum ausmalen!

Colour your own rainbow!

Und jetzt bist Du dran!

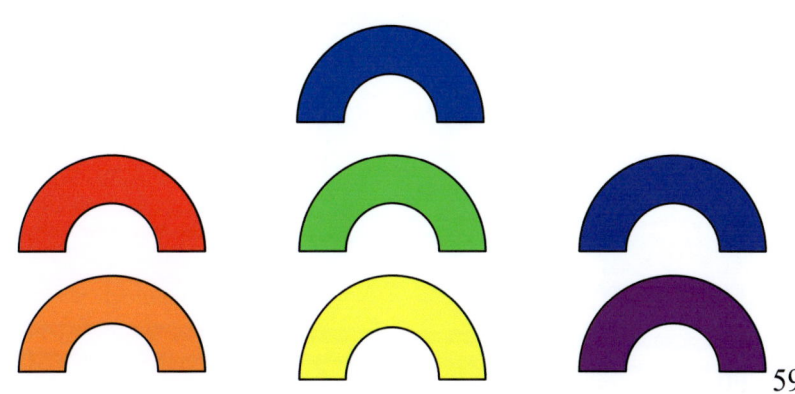

Rainbows for parents:
www.eo.ucar.edu/rainbows

Regenbögen zum Nachlesen:
www.wikipedia.de